VIRGINIA

The Old Dominion

BY
JOHN HAMILTON

Abdo & Daughters
An imprint of Abdo Publishing | abdopublishing.com

abdopublishing.com

Published by ABDO Publishing, a division of ABDO, PO Box 398166, Minneapolis, Minnesota 55439. Copyright © 2017 by Abdo Consulting Group, Inc. International copyrights reserved in all countries. No part of this book may be reproduced in any form without written permission from the publisher. ABDO & Daughters™ is a trademark and logo of ABDO Publishing.

Printed in the United States of America, North Mankato, Minnesota.
072016
092016

Editor: Sue Hamilton   **Contributing Editor:** Bridget O'Brien
Graphic Design: Sue Hamilton
Cover Art Direction: Candice Keimig   **Cover Photo Selection:** Neil Klinepier
Cover Photo: iStock
Interior Images: Alamy, Albert Gallatin Hoit, AP, Berni Nonemacher, Getty, Gilbert Stuart, Granger Collection, iStock, Independence National Historical Park-Charles Willson Peale, John Hamilton, Library of Congress, Mile High Maps, Minden Pictures, Mountain High Maps, National Park Service-Sidney E. King & Keith Rocco, National Portrait Gallery-London, One Mile Up, Rembrandt Peale, U.S. Forest Service, U.S. Navy-Christopher B. Stoltz, University of Virginia, White House Historical Association-John Vanderlyn & Joseph H. Bush, William James Hubbard, & Wikimedia.

Statistics: *State and City Populations*, U.S. Census Bureau, July 1, 2015 estimates; *Land and Water Area*, U.S. Census Bureau, 2010 Census, MAF/TIGER database; *State Temperature Extremes*, NOAA National Climatic Data Center; *Climatology and Average Annual Precipitation*, NOAA National Climatic Data Center, 1980-2015 statewide averages; *State Highest and Lowest Points*, NOAA National Geodetic Survey.

Websites: To learn more about the United States, visit booklinks.abdopublishing.com. These links are routinely monitored and updated to provide the most current information available.

Cataloging-in-Publication Data

Names: Hamilton, John, 1959- author.
Title: Virginia / by John Hamilton.
Description: Minneapolis, MN : Abdo Publishing, [2017] | Series: The United
    States of America | Includes index.
Identifiers: LCCN 2015957744 | ISBN 9781680783490 (lib. bdg.) |
    ISBN 9781680774535 (ebook)
Subjects: LCSH: Virginia--Juvenile literature.
Classification: DDC 975.5--dc23
LC record available at http://lccn.loc.gov/2015957744

CONTENTS

The Old Dominion 4

Quick Facts 6

Geography 8

Climate and Weather 12

Plants and Animals. 14

History. 18

Did You Know? 24

People 26

Cities 30

Transportation 34

Natural Resources. 36

Industry 38

Sports. 40

Entertainment 42

Timeline. 44

Glossary 46

Index 48

THE OLD DOMINION

Virginia is a state with one foot in the past and the other planted firmly in the future. It is a Southern state with forested mountains, rolling plains, and steep valleys. It also contains some of the fastest-growing cities in America. Sleepy small towns are just a short drive from bustling urban areas that surround the nation's capital of Washington, DC, just across the Potomac River to the northeast.

Virginia was one of the original 13 American colonies. Important battles were fought in the state during the Revolutionary War and the Civil War. Many battlefields have been preserved to remind people of the past. The homes of Presidents George Washington and Thomas Jefferson are also in Virginia.

Virginia was one of the oldest overseas dominions, or territories, of England. In the mid-1600s, Virginia remained loyal to England's King Charles II. That is why Virginia's nickname is "The Old Dominion."

Monticello, Thomas Jefferson's home.

QUICK FACTS

Name: Virginia is named in honor of England's Queen Elizabeth I (1533-1603). She was often called the Virgin Queen because she never married.

State Capital: Richmond, population 220,289

Date of Statehood: June 25, 1788 (10th state)

Population: 8,382,993 (12th-most populous state)

Area (Total Land and Water): 42,775 square miles (110,787 sq km), 35th-largest state

Largest City: Virginia Beach, population 452,745

Nickname: The Old Dominion

Motto: *Sic Semper Tyrannis* (Thus Always to Tyrants)

State Bird: Northern Cardinal

State Flower: White Flowering Dogwood

State Tree: White Flowering Dogwood

State Fossil: Chesapecten jeffersonius (scallop fossil)

Mount Rogers

Atlantic Ocean

George Washington

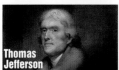
Thomas Jefferson

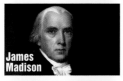
James Madison

James Monroe

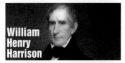
William Henry Harrison

John Tyler

Zachary Taylor

Woodrow Wilson

State Song: "Carry Me Back to Old Virginia"; "Sweet Virginia Breeze"; "Our Great Virginia"

Highest Point: Mount Rogers, 5,729 feet (1,746 m)

Lowest Point: Atlantic Ocean, 0 feet (0 m)

Average July High Temperature: 86°F (30°C)

Record High Temperature: 110°F (43°C), in Balcony Falls on July 15, 1954

Average January Low Temperature: 25°F (-4°C)

Record Low Temperature: -30°F (-34°C), in Mountain Lake on January 21, 1985

Average Annual Precipitation: 44 inches (112 cm)

Number of U.S. Senators: 2

Number of U.S. Representatives: 11

U.S. Presidents Born in Virginia: George Washington (1732-1799); Thomas Jefferson (1743-1826); James Madison (1751-1836); James Monroe (1758-1831); William Henry Harrison (1773-1841); John Tyler (1790-1862); Zachary Taylor (1784-1850); Woodrow Wilson (1856-1924)

U.S. Postal Service Abbreviation: VA

GEOGRAPHY

Virginia is part of the Upper South region of the United States. It lies along the eastern seaboard. It covers 42,775 square miles (110,787 sq km) of land and water, which makes it the 35th-largest state. It is roughly 427 miles (687 km) long at its widest point along its southern border. From north to south, it measures about 202 miles (325 km) from its southern border to its most northern point.

Bordering Virginia to the south are the states of North Carolina and Tennessee. To the northwest are Kentucky and West Virginia. To the northeast are Maryland and Washington, DC. Virginia's eastern border is formed by Chesapeake Bay and the Atlantic Ocean.

The Potomac River forms the border between Virginia and Maryland.

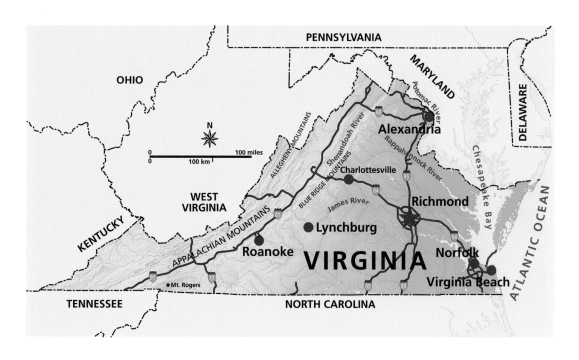

Virginia's total land and water area is 42,775 square miles (110,787 sq km). It is the 35th-largest state. The state capital is Richmond.

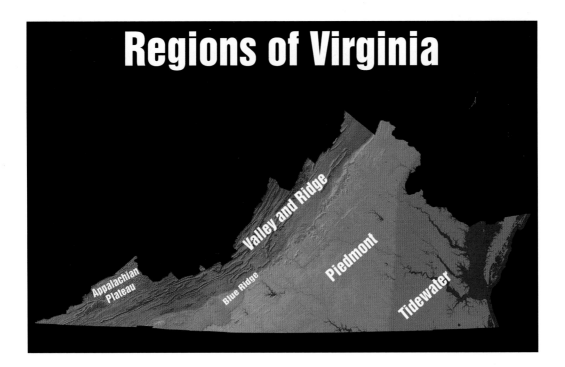

Regions of Virginia

Virginia has five main regions. They include the Tidewater, Piedmont, Blue Ridge, Valley and Ridge, and Appalachian Plateau regions.

The Tidewater region in the east occupies about one-third of Virginia. It gets its name from the tides in Chesapeake Bay and the Atlantic Ocean. Chesapeake Bay is the largest estuary in the United States. Major rivers that flow into the bay include the James, Rappahannock, and Potomac Rivers.

West of the Tidewater is the Piedmont. It is Virginia's largest region. Moving westward, the land gently rises in elevation. There are rolling hills and valleys with farmland. Mountains can be seen rising to the west.

Between the Piedmont and the Tidewater is a natural border called the Fall Line. The land rises abruptly. As rivers pass over the area, there are many rapids and waterfalls.

West of the Piedmont are the Blue Ridge Mountains. They are part of the Appalachian Mountains. They rose up hundreds of millions of years ago. From a distance, the forested mountainsides appear to have a blue tint. Virginia's highest point is in this region. It is Mount Rogers, which rises 5,729 feet (1,746 m) high.

West of the Blue Ridge Mountains is the Valley and Ridge region. There are many narrow valleys separated by mountains. From space, it appears as if a giant comb has been dragged across the landscape. The beautiful and fertile Shenandoah Valley, as well as the Allegheny Mountains, are in this region.

In the far western part of Virginia is the Appalachian Plateau. These forested highlands include small, narrow valleys. There are also many coal mines in this region.

Shenandoah Valley

CLIMATE AND
WEATHER

Eastern Virginia has a humid subtropical climate. West of the Blue Ridge Mountains, there is a humid continental climate. In general, the state has warm, humid summers and mild winters.

Weather in the eastern Tidewater region is affected by the Atlantic Ocean. It is usually mild and humid. Hurricanes rarely strike the Chesapeake Bay area. When they do move over Virginia, they usually weaken before reaching heavily populated cities.

A ballplayer watches a rainbow form as a storm clears in Winchester, Virginia.

Snow blankets the Marine Corps Memorial in Arlington, Virginia. The state typically has mild winters.

Virginia's mountains can have frost and snow in winter. The state's record cold temperature occurred on January 21, 1985, in Mountain Lake. On that day, the thermometer sank to -30°F (-34°C). Virginia's record high temperature is 110°F (43°C). It occurred on July 15, 1954, in the town of Balcony Falls.

Statewide, Virginia's average annual precipitation is 44 inches (112 cm). When weather systems from the Atlantic Ocean drift over the state, clouds rise when they meet the eastern slopes of the Blue Ridge Mountains. Moisture condenses and falls as rain or snow. Clouds blowing from the west drop moisture on the westward-facing slopes of the Appalachian Mountains. The New River and Shenandoah Valleys are between the mountain chains. They are the driest parts of the state.

CLIMATE AND WEATHER

PLANTS AND ANIMALS

Virginia has nearly 16 million acres (6.5 million ha) of forestland. That is about 63 percent of the state's land area. The majority of the forests are privately owned. However, hundreds of thousands of acres of forestland are publicly owned, managed, and protected. The state has 2 national forests, 24 state forests, plus beautiful Shenandoah National Park in northwestern Virginia.

Shenandoah National Park

White Flowering
Dogwood

The forests of the western mountains include broadleaf deciduous trees such as oak and hickory. Pines dominate the central Piedmont and Tidewater regions, although there are some hardwood deciduous trees. Other common trees found in Virginia include ash, beech, locust, maple, poplar, sweet gum, and black walnut. The state tree of Virginia is the white flowering dogwood.

Wildflowers add a splash of color to Virginia's woodlands and meadows. Wildflowers that are native to the state include bluebells, bloodroot, phlox, cardinal flower, Jack-in-the-pulpit, spiderwort, and sweet flag. The official state flower is the white flowering dogwood. Virginia is the only state that has the same plant for its official flower and tree.

PLANTS AND ANIMALS

Deer are common in Virginia.

With its many different ecosystems, from ocean shores to mountaintops, Virginia is home to a large variety of wildlife. Mammals found roaming the state's forests include black bears, white-tailed deer, beavers, bobcats, coyotes, muskrats, opossums, rabbits, raccoons, skunks, and woodchucks. Black bears live mainly in the mountains, but can sometimes be found in swampy coastal areas. Elk used to live all over the state, but they died out from overhunting in the 1800s. Herds of elk have been reintroduced in southwestern Virginia.

Virginia has many bird-friendly habitats. Several species of ducks, geese, and swans pass through the state when they migrate. Coastal marshes and beaches are home to egrets, sandpipers, plovers, gulls, pelicans, great blue herons, and terns. Farther inland, birdwatchers can spot doves, eagles, blackbirds, finches, grouse, red-tailed hawks, ospreys, great horned owls, quail, sparrows, wild turkeys, and downy woodpeckers. There are many kinds of songbirds, including blue jays, mourning doves, American robins, red-winged blackbirds, and Carolina chickadees. The official state bird is the northern cardinal.

Many reptiles and amphibians can be found scrambling and hopping over the ground in Virginia. Just a few of them include American bullfrogs, black-bellied salamanders, broad-headed skinks, leopard frogs, and eastern painted turtles. Several species of snakes are native to the state. A few are venomous, including timber rattlesnakes, cottonmouths, and copperheads. Like all snakes, these reptiles are helpful to the state's ecosystems. They eat rodent pests such as mice, voles, and rats.

Virginia's inland lakes, rivers, and offshore waters are teeming with many kinds of fish. They include largemouth and smallmouth bass, bluegill, sunfish, walleye, muskellunge, northern pike, rainbow trout, catfish, marlin, tuna, and wahoo.

Great Blue Heron

HISTORY

The first people to settle in the Virginia area were Paleo-Indians. These early ancestors of today's Native Americans were nomads who hunted large animals such as mammoths and bison. They came to Virginia 10,000 to 12,000 years ago, after the Ice Age glaciers melted.

By the 1600s, many Native American tribes had established themselves in Virginia. They were dominated by a powerful Algonquian-speaking group of Indians called the Powhatan Confederacy. Other Native Americans in the area included the Iroquois, Siouan, and Cherokee.

In the 1600s, Chief Powhatan was leader of the Virginia area's Powhatan Confederacy.

English settlers arrived in Virginia in 1607, naming their settlement Jamestown for England's King James I. To survive, they traded with local Indians for food.

In the 1580s, English adventurer Sir Walter Raleigh and others sent expeditions to explore the coast of present-day Virginia. The area was named Virginia in honor of England's Queen Elizabeth I. She was called the Virgin Queen because she never married. The English tried to start colonies in the late 1500s, but failed.

In 1607, English settlers built a wooden fort along the James River near the marshy entrance to Chesapeake Bay. They called the fort Jamestown. It became the first permanent English settlement in North America.

The settlers were unprepared for the hardships they faced. Many died of illness and starvation. Thanks to the leadership of Captain John Smith, the settlement survived. More colonists arrived from England, and Jamestown continued to grow.

Tobacco quickly became an important crop to the Virginia colonists.

As Jamestown grew, other settlements in Virginia sprang up. The colonists hoped to find gold in the new land, but they cultivated something almost as valuable: tobacco. It grew well in Virginia's soil, and the colonists received good prices for it in England.

African slaves and servants were first brought to Virginia in 1619 to work on the farms. This made tobacco even more profitable. In addition to tobacco, sugar and rice were grown. Many fortunes were made. That same year, the colony elected its first representative government. It was called the House of Burgesses.

The English settlement of Virginia continued. Pioneers pushed west and north, even beyond the Appalachian Mountains. There were conflicts with Native Americans, who resisted the loss of their lands. Thousands of Indians were killed due to warfare and diseases brought by the settlers, such as smallpox and measles.

In the mid-1700s, many Virginians had grown angry about English taxes and laws. They noisily demanded a voice in the British government. "No taxation without representation" was their rallying cry. Britain's King George III refused. The unfair taxes and laws continued.

By the 1770s, the colonists were ready to cut ties with Great Britain. In 1775, Virginia joined the other 12 American colonies and fought the Revolutionary War (1775-1783).

In 1776, Virginian Thomas Jefferson wrote the Declaration of Independence. Another Virginian, George Washington, became the commander of America's Continental Army. In 1781, Washington's forces, with help from the French navy, beat the English army at Yorktown, Virginia. The battle won the war for America's freedom from British rule.

General George Washington and his French ally, Lieutenant General Rochambeau, accepted the surrender of British troops after the siege of Yorktown in October 1781. The battle won the war for America's freedom.

After the Revolutionary War, Virginia became the 10th state on June 25, 1788. In 1789, George Washington became the first president of the United States. Virginia was a much larger state than it is today. In 1792, the territory of Kentucky split from Virginia and became its own state.

Virginia grew rapidly in the early 1800s. Roads and railroads began crisscrossing the state. That made it easier to transport farm products and other goods to big markets in the north.

Slavery continued to divide Virginia, and the country. Large plantation owners wanted cheap labor to plant and harvest tobacco and other crops. The large farms were not as profitable without slaves.

Abraham Lincoln became president in 1861. He opposed slavery and wanted it abolished. Virginia joined 10 other Southern states and seceded, or left, the Union. They called themselves the Confederate States of America. Richmond, Virginia, eventually became the Confederacy's capital.

A slave auction in Virginia in 1861. Slavery divided the United States, and led Virginia and 10 other Southern states to secede from the Union in 1861.

Richmond, Virginia, was in ruins by the end of the Civil War.

Virginians were torn over their loyalties. The northwestern part of the state broke away and remained in the Union. It became the state of West Virginia. Many bloody battles were fought in Virginia during the Civil War (1861-1865). By the time the South surrendered, much of the state was in ruins. The slaves were freed, and it took decades to rebuild the shattered state.

During the 1900s, Virginia modernized. Railroads, logging, textiles, and the coal industry helped the economy. High-tech industries and military bases were built in the state. Today, northern Virginia has close ties to the Washington, DC, metropolitan area. The United States government remains a major employer. Virginia is a more racially integrated place, and many people have moved from the country to large cities.

DID YOU KNOW?

• Captain John Smith and Pocahontas did not have a romance, even though popular folklore—and a Disney movie—claim they did. In 1607, Smith was the leader of Virginia's Jamestown settlement. He wrote that one day, while hunting for food, he was ambushed and taken prisoner by Powhatan Native Americans. The Powhatans were alarmed at the growing number of English settlers. Smith was about to be killed, but the Powhatan chief's 12-year-old daughter defended him. The girl's name was Pocahontas. She convinced her father to set the English captain free. Years later, Pocahontas married another English settler, John Rolfe.

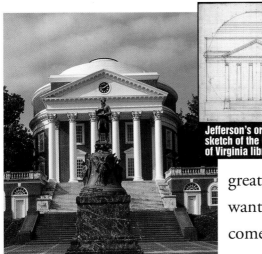

Jefferson's original sketch of the University of Virginia library.

• In the early 1800s, President Thomas Jefferson helped design the University of Virginia's campus in Charlottesville, Virginia. Jefferson placed great importance on education. He wanted students from all over America to come to the university "and drink of the cup of knowledge." Jefferson's home of Monticello is nearby.

• Arlington National Cemetery is a military cemetery in northern Virginia. It was established in 1864 during the Civil War. It is near the shores of the Potomac River, across from Washington, DC. The cemetery is built on the grounds of Arlington House, the family home of Confederate General Robert E. Lee. About 400,000 people are buried at Arlington National Cemetery, representing every war that the United States has fought. Presidents John F. Kennedy and William Howard Taft are also buried there. One of the most famous memorials is the Tomb of the Unknown Soldier. It contains the unidentified remains of service members from World War I, World War II, the Korean War, and the Vietnam War.

DID YOU KNOW?

PEOPLE

George Washington (1732-1799) was the first president of the United States. He served from 1789-1797. Washington was born in Westmoreland County, Virginia. The son of a wealthy planter, he grew up to be a well-mannered Virginia gentleman and an excellent horseman. He became a land surveyor at age 16. He learned military tactics while fighting in the French and Indian War (1754-1763). During the Revolutionary War (1775-1783), Washington was the commander-in-chief of the Continental Army. After the war, he led a group of politicians, called the Founding Fathers, in creating the United States Constitution. After serving as president, Washington retired to his plantation at Mount Vernon, Virginia. Today, he is often referred to as the father of the United States.

Thomas Jefferson (1743-1826) was the third president of the United States. He was born in Albemarle County in Virginia. He grew up to become a wealthy, well-educated landowner. He was the main author of America's Declaration of Independence.

After the Revolutionary War, Jefferson served as a diplomat in France, and then as the first United States secretary of state under President George Washington. He served as vice president under President John Adams. He was then elected the third president of the United States. He served two terms, from 1801 to 1809. After serving as president, Jefferson retired to his home at Monticello, near Charlottesville, Virginia. Because he knew the importance of a well-educated public, he founded the University of Virginia in Charlottesville in 1819.

Robert E. Lee (1807-1870) was the commander of the Confederate Army of Northern Virginia during the Civil War (1861-1865). He was the South's most successful and popular general. During the war's early years, he managed to find ways to win battles, even against overwhelming odds. He was a former United States Army officer, but he believed he owed his loyalty to his home state of Virginia. He left the Army to fight for the Confederacy. Lee was born in Westmoreland County, Virginia.

Arthur Ashe (1943-1993) was a top-ranked tennis player born in Richmond, Virginia. Many believe he was one of the greatest tennis players of all time. He won the US Open in 1968, the Australian Open in 1970, and Wimbledon in 1975. To date, he is the only African American to win all three of these men's singles titles. Ashe also helped children and promoted civil rights. He contracted HIV after a tainted blood transfusion in the 1980s. Until his death in 1993, he educated people about AIDS and HIV.

Booker T. Washington (1856-1915) was born a slave on a tobacco plantation in Hale's Ford, Virginia. After the Civil War, he worked his way through school. He became a leading spokesman and educator who fought for civil rights for African Americans. He believed in the power of education to help people improve their lives. Starting in 1881, he led the Tuskegee Institute, an all-black university in Alabama. The school became famous for the quality of its students.

Sandra Bullock (1964-) is an Academy Award-winning actress who is one of the biggest stars in Hollywood. Born in Arlington, Virginia, she started acting in school plays. She also studied dance and music. One of her first big breaks was in 1994's action movie *Speed*. She has since gone on to star in many blockbusters, including *While You Were Sleeping*, *Miss Congeniality*, and *Gravity*. She won a Best Actress Academy Award in 2010 for her work in *The Blind Side*. She is also a successful film producer.

CITIES

Richmond is the capital of Virginia. Its population is about 220,289. It is located in the east-central part of the state, along the James River. During the Civil War, Richmond was the capital of the Confederate States of America. Large parts of the city were burned and destroyed during the fighting. Today, the city has bounced back. There are many state and federal government offices. Other important employers include high-tech and biotechnology companies, manufacturing, law firms, banks, and health care facilities. The Virginia Museum of Fine Arts is one of the best art museums in the country. It contains more than 33,000 works of art from all over the world, from ancient statues to modern paintings. Historic St. John's Church is where Revolutionary War politician Patrick Henry gave his fiery "Give me liberty, or give me death!" speech.

Virginia Beach is the largest city in the state of Virginia. Its population is about 452,745. It is located on the Atlantic Ocean coast, near the mouth of Chesapeake Bay. It is a popular beach resort community, but there are also large corporations, universities, and military bases. The Virginia Aquarium & Marine Science Center is home to more than 300 species of marine animals, including harbor seals, loggerhead turtles, river otters, and sand tiger sharks.

Alexandria is in northeastern Virginia, along the shores of the Potomac River and just a few miles from Washington, DC. Its population is about 153,511. Many people who live in Alexandria work in the nation's capital. The city's top employer is the United States government, especially the Department of Defense. Alexandria is famous for its "Old Town" historic center. There are many popular restaurants, antique shops, and theaters.

Norfolk is the second-largest city in Virginia. Its population is about 246,393. It is part of a region in southeastern Virginia called Hampton Roads, which is home to more than 1 million people. It also includes a large sea harbor, where the United States Navy's Naval Station Norfolk is located. It is the largest naval base in the world. Major employers include the military, sea shipping, education, and government.

Charlottesville is in northwestern Virginia, just east of the Blue Ridge Mountains. Its population is about 46,597. The city's biggest employers are education, health care, banking, and government. The University of Virginia was founded in 1819. It enrolls nearly 22,000 students yearly. Nearby is historic Monticello, the home and plantation of President Thomas Jefferson. The building's familiar west side is on the reverse of U.S. five-cent coins.

Roanoke is in southwestern Virginia, along the banks of the Roanoke River and just west of the Blue Ridge Mountains. Its population is about 99,897. The city's economy depends largely on retail stores, health care, transportation, and manufacturing. Roanoke is located near the Blue Ridge Parkway. It is a 469-mile (755-km) road that meanders through the stunning beauty of the Blue Ridge Mountains.

Lynchburg is in west-central Virginia, in the foothills of the Blue Ridge Mountains and along the shores of the James River. Its population is about 79,812. Lynchburg has a thriving business community. Major employers include health care, education, energy, banking, and retail. Nearby is Appomattox Court House National Historical Park, the site where General Robert E. Lee surrendered the Confederate Army at the end of the Civil War in 1865.

TRANSPORTATION

Since the late 1600s, Virginia has depended on Chesapeake Bay and its river systems for an easy way to transport goods. Virginia's Hampton Roads is both a metropolitan area and the name of a large harbor near the mouth of Chesapeake Bay. The Port of Virginia is one of the most active port areas in the world. Its busy docks handle nearly 20 million tons (18 million metric tons) of general cargo yearly.

There are nine freight railroads in Virginia hauling cargo on 3,215 miles (5,174 km) of track that crisscross the state. Coal is by far the most common product carried by train, followed by chemicals, paper products, scrap, plus sand and gravel. Passengers are whisked across Virginia by several Amtrak lines, as well as busy commuter rail services to major metropolitan areas.

Port of Virginia

Washington Dulles International Airport is one of the busiest airports in Virginia. On an average day, about 60,000 passengers pass through it.

There are 74,748 miles (120,295 km) of public roadways in Virginia, including more than 1,100 miles (1,770 km) of interstate highways connecting major cities. There are more than 20,900 bridges in the state. The most spectacular is the 23-mile (37-km) -long Chesapeake Bay Bridge-Tunnel. It crosses lower Chesapeake Bay, connecting Virginia's Eastern Shore with Virginia Beach, in the Hampton Roads area. It includes two long tunnels that travel under the bay's main shipping channels.

The busiest airports in Virginia are Washington Dulles International Airport, Ronald Reagan Washington National Airport, Norfolk International Airport, Richmond International Airport, and Newport News-Williamsburg International Airport. Washington Dulles handles more than 21.5 million passengers yearly.

NATURAL RESOURCES

There are about 44,700 farms in Virginia. The average farm size is 181 acres (73 ha). In total, Virginia's farmland covers 8.1 million acres (3.3 million ha) of land. That is about 32 percent of the state's total land area.

The most valuable crops raised in Virginia include hay, soybeans, corn for livestock, and wheat. Tobacco was once a big cash crop in Virginia, but other crops now make more money. Even so, the state is one of the top producers of tobacco in the country. Other important farm products include chickens, turkeys, cattle, dairy products, tomatoes, apples, grapes, peanuts, potatoes, sweet corn, peaches, and cucumbers.

Hay is harvested on a farm near Dayton, Virginia. Hay is one of the state's most valuable crops.

A Christmas tree farm near Berryville, Virginia. The state is a top producer of Christmas trees.

About 63 percent of Virginia is covered by forests. The forest industry adds about $17 billion to the state's economy each year, which supports more than 103,000 jobs. Logging produces products such as plywood, paper, and furniture. Virginia is also a top producer of Christmas trees.

Coal is mined in southwestern Virginia. Production has declined in recent years. Many power plants that burn coal to make energy have switched to cheaper natural gas. Other products mined in Virginia include crushed stone, plus sand and gravel.

Commercial fishing in Chesapeake Bay brings in big catches of crabs, oysters, and clams. Fish caught in the Atlantic Ocean include menhaden, flounder, and bass.

NATURAL RESOURCES

INDUSTRY

Virginia factories produce many kinds of products. Manufacturing accounts for about 10 percent of the state's economy. Important industries include aerospace, food processing, energy, transportation, plastics, and chemicals.

Because Virginia is so close to Washington, DC, the United States government is a major employer in the state. Several government agencies have headquarters in Virginia. They include the Central Intelligence Agency (CIA), the Department of Defense (headquartered in the Pentagon), the National Science Foundation, the United States Geological Survey, and the United States Patent and Trademark Office.

Naval Station Norfolk is the largest naval base in the world.

Virginia's Hampton Roads area is home to many military bases and facilities. The largest naval base in the world is Naval Station Norfolk, in Norfolk, Virginia. Virginia's military bases support thousands of jobs and greatly boost the state's economy.

Like many states, Virginia's service industry has become very important in recent years. Instead of making products, service industry companies sell services to other businesses and consumers. It includes businesses such as banking, financial services, health care, insurance, restaurants, and tourism. About 67 percent of people working in Virginia have jobs in the service industry.

One very important service industry in Virginia is tourism. People come to the state to relax on the sandy beaches, hike in the Blue Ridge Mountains, or see historic sites such as Thomas Jefferson's home at Monticello. Each year, visitors spend about $23 billion in Virginia. That is enough to support more than 222,600 jobs.

INDUSTRY

SPORTS

Virginia has no professional major league sports teams. Many Virginians are fans of teams from neighboring Washington, DC. They include the Washington Redskins (football), the Washington Nationals (baseball), the Washington Wizards (basketball), and the Washington Capitals (hockey). In addition, there are several popular minor league sports teams that play football, baseball, hockey, and soccer.

The University of Virginia, in Charlottesville, has 11 men's and 12 women's varsity teams. The teams are called the Virginia Cavaliers. They are also called the Wahoos because of their rallying cry, "Wa-hoo-wa!" The Virginia Tech Hokies represent Virginia Tech, in Blacksburg. There are 10 men's and 10 women's varsity teams.

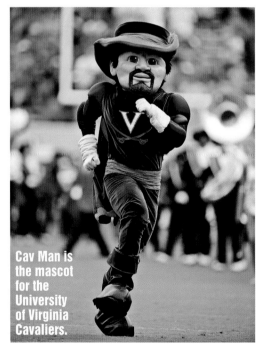

Cav Man is the mascot for the University of Virginia Cavaliers.

HokieBird is the mascot for the Virginia Tech Hokies.

Martinsville Speedway

Many people take advantage of Virginia's beautiful scenery while participating in outdoor sports. There are hundreds of golf courses throughout the state. Hiking and biking trails wind through Virginia's mountains, forests, and rolling hills. Virginia is home to 544 miles (875 km) of the famous Appalachian Trail.

People enjoy yacht racing, fishing, diving, and snorkeling on Chesapeake Bay and the Atlantic Ocean. On the state's rivers and lakes, canoeing, kayaking, and fishing are popular.

For car racing fans, there are several tracks in and near Virginia that host NASCAR events. The Martinsville Speedway, in Ridgeway, opened in 1947. The 0.526-mile (.847-km) track has long straightaways and challenging narrow banks.

ENTERTAINMENT

Virginia has many theaters, ballet troupes, and classical orchestras scattered throughout the state. Music festivals and museums are also popular. Wolf Trap National Park for the Performing Arts, in Fairfax County, is the only national park set aside for theater and musical performances.

Virginia is filled with historic sites. One of the most popular is Mount Vernon, the beloved home of President George Washington. Located on the shores of the Potomac River, it is just 17 miles (27 km) south of Washington, DC. Mount Vernon contains Washington's 21-room mansion, plus an extensive garden landscape, which Washington designed. Both President Washington and First Lady Martha Washington are entombed on the estate. There is also a memorial to the African American slaves and servants who worked at Mount Vernon.

Tourists flock to Mount Vernon, George and Martha Washington's historic home.

Manassas National Battlefield Park, in Prince William County, preserves the site where two major Civil War battles were fought. Today, more than 900,000 visitors come each year to learn about the war.

The city of Williamsburg was founded in 1632. It was Virginia's capital from 1699 to 1780. Today, historic Colonial Williamsburg is a 301-acre (122-ha) living history museum. Visitors can tour 88 original restored buildings, and learn from hundreds of reenactors who demonstrate what life was like in the 1700s.

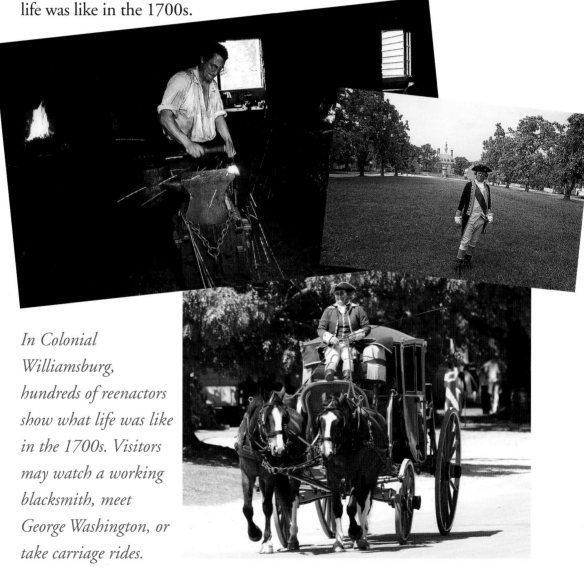

In Colonial Williamsburg, hundreds of reenactors show what life was like in the 1700s. Visitors may watch a working blacksmith, meet George Washington, or take carriage rides.

TIMELINE

10,000-8,000 BC—The first Paleo-Indians arrive in the Virginia area.

1580s—Virginia is named for England's Queen Elizabeth I.

1600s—Native Americans established in Virginia include the Powhatan Confederacy, plus members of the Iroquois, Siouan, and Cherokee tribes.

1607—Jamestown is founded. It is the first permanent English settlement in North America.

1619—The House of Burgesses is created. The first African slaves arrive.

1775—The Revolutionary War begins.

1776—Virginian Thomas Jefferson writes the Declaration of Independence.

1781—Virginian George Washington leads the Continental Army to defeat the British at Yorktown.

1788—Virginia becomes the 10th state in the Union.

1831—A slave rebellion led by Nat Turner kills more than 55 people. After the rebellion is put down, more than 100 slaves are killed after being accused of supporting the uprising.

1861—The Civil War begins. Virginia joins the Confederacy.

1865—General Robert E. Lee surrenders at Appomattox Court House, Virginia, marking the end of the Civil War.

1989—Lawrence Douglas Wilder becomes the first African American elected governor of Virginia.

2001—Five terrorists hijack and fly a plane into the Pentagon on September 11, killing 184 innocent people.

2011—A rare strong earthquake rattles north-central Virginia, causing minor-to-moderate widespread damage to buildings in the area.

2016—The University of Virginia men's varsity tennis team wins the NCAA national championship.

GLOSSARY

COLONY

A group of people who settle in a distant territory but remain citizens of their native country.

CONSTITUTION

A set of laws that establish the rules and principles of a country or organization.

DECIDUOUS

A tree or other plant that sheds its leaves each autumn.

ECOSYSTEM

A biological community of animals, plants, and bacteria who live together in the same physical or chemical environment.

ESTUARY

The mouth of a freshwater river, where it meets the sea and mixes with saltwater. Estuaries mark the transition zone between river and ocean ecosystems. Many kinds of unique plants and animals live in estuaries.

FOUNDING FATHERS

The men who participated in the Constitutional Convention in 1787, especially the ones who signed the finished Constitution. The term also sometimes refers to the men who signed the Declaration of Independence in 1776.

HIV

A virus that causes AIDS, a condition in which the body's immune system fails and fatal diseases and infections are easily caught. HIV stands for "human immunodeficiency virus." AIDS stands for "acquired immune deficiency syndrome."

Ice Age

A period of time in which huge, slow-moving sheets of ice grow and shrink as the climate changes. During the Ice Age, some glaciers covered entire regions and measured more than one mile (1.6 km) thick.

NASCAR

National Association for Stock Car Auto Racing. A popular sporting event with races held across the United States. The Martinsville Speedway in Ridgeway, Virginia, hosts many NASCAR races.

Piedmont

A large region that is adjacent to mountains. The word *piedmont* is from an Italian word that means "at the foot of the mountains."

Plantation

A large farm where crops such as tobacco, rice, and sugar are raised by people who live on the estate. In Virginia's early history, African slaves were forced to work on large tobacco plantations.

Powhatan Confederacy

A group of about 30 Native American peoples who lived in Virginia's Tidewater region. Their leader was also named Powhatan. In the early 1600s, European settlers met Powhatan and his daughter, who was named Pocahontas.

INDEX

A

Academy Award 29
Adams, John 27
AIDS 28
Alabama 29
Albemarle County, VA 27
Alexandria, VA 31
Allegheny Mountains 11
America (*see* United States)
Amtrak 34
Appalachian Mountains 11, 13, 20
Appalachian Plateau region 10, 11
Appalachian Trail 41
Appomattox Court House National Historical Park 33
Arlington, VA 29
Arlington House 25
Arlington National Cemetery 25
Army, U.S. 28
Ashe, Arthur 28
Atlantic Ocean 8, 10, 12, 13, 31, 37, 41
Australian Open 28

B

Balcony Falls, VA 13
Best Actress 29
Blacksburg, VA 40
Blind Side, The 29
Blue Ridge Mountains 11, 12, 13, 32, 33, 39
Blue Ridge Parkway 33
Blue Ridge region 10, 11
Bullock, Sandra 29

C

Central Intelligence Agency (CIA) 38
Charles II, King of England 4
Charlottesville, VA 25, 27, 32, 40
Cherokee (tribe) 18
Chesapeake Bay 8, 10, 12, 19, 31, 34, 35, 37, 41
Chesapeake Bay Bridge-Tunnel 35
Civil War 4, 23, 25, 28, 29, 30, 33, 43
Colonial Williamsburg 43
Confederacy (*see* Confederate States of America)
Confederate Army of Northern Virginia 28, 33
Confederate States of America 22, 28, 30
Constitution, U.S. 26
Continental Army 21, 26

D

Declaration of Independence 21, 27
Department of Defense 31, 38
Disney 24

E

Eastern Shore 35
Elizabeth I, Queen of England 19
England 4, 19, 20

F

Fairfax County 42
Fall Line 10
Founding Fathers 26
France 27
French and Indian War 26

G

George III, King of Great Britain 21
Gravity 29
Great Britain 21

H

Hale's Ford, VA 29
Hampton Roads 32, 34, 35, 39
Henry, Patrick 30
HIV 28
Hollywood 29
House of Burgesses 20

I

Ice Age 18
Iroquois (tribe) 18

J

James River 10, 19, 30, 33
Jamestown, VA 19, 20, 24
Jefferson, Thomas 4, 21, 25, 27, 32, 39

K

Kennedy, John F. 25
Kentucky 8, 22
Korean War 25

L

Lee, Robert E. 25, 28, 33
Lincoln, Abraham 22
Lynchburg, VA 33

M

Manassas National Battlefield Park 43
Martinsville Speedway 41
Maryland 8
Miss Congeniality 29
Monticello 25, 27, 32, 39
Mount Vernon 26, 42
Mountain Lake, VA 13

N

NASCAR 41
National Science Foundation 38
Naval Station Norfolk 32, 39
Navy, U.S. 32
New River Valley 13
Newport News-Williamsburg International Airport 35
Norfolk, VA 32, 39
Norfolk International Airport 35
North America 19
North Carolina 8

O

Old Dominion, The 4
Old Town 31

P

Paleo-Indians 18
Pentagon 38
Piedmont region 10, 11, 15
Pocahontas 24
Port of Virginia 34
Potomac River 4, 10, 25, 31, 42
Powhatan Confederacy (tribe) 18, 24
Prince William County 43

R

Raleigh, Walter 19
Rappahannock River 10
Revolutionary War 4, 21, 22, 26, 27, 30
Richmond, VA 22, 28, 30
Richmond International Airport 35
Ridgeway, VA 41
Roanoke, VA 33
Roanoke River 33
Rogers, Mount 11
Rolfe, John 24
Ronald Reagan Washington National Airport 35

S

Shenandoah National Park 14
Shenandoah Valley 11, 13
Siouan (tribe) 18
Smith, John 19, 24
South 23, 28
Speed 29
St. John's Church 30

T

Taft, William Howard 25
Tennessee 8
Tidewater region 10, 12, 15
Tomb of the Unknown Soldier 25
Tuskegee Institute 29

U

Union 22, 23
United States 4, 8, 10, 21, 22, 23, 25, 26, 27, 28, 31, 32, 38
United States Geological Survey 38
United States Patent and Trademark Office 38
University of Virginia 25, 27, 32, 40
Upper South (U.S. region) 8
US Open 28

V

Valley and Ridge region 10, 11
Vietnam War 25
Virgin Queen (*see* Elizabeth I, Queen of England)
Virginia Aquarium & Marine Science Center 31
Virginia Beach, VA 31, 35
Virginia Cavaliers 40
Virginia Museum of Fine Arts 30
Virginia Tech 40
Virginia Tech Hokies 40

W

Wahoos 40
Washington, Booker T. 29
Washington, DC 4, 8, 23, 25, 31, 38, 40, 42
Washington, George 4, 21, 22, 26, 27, 42
Washington, Martha 42
Washington Capitals 40
Washington Dulles International Airport 35
Washington Nationals 40
Washington Redskins 40
Washington Wizards 40
West Virginia 8, 23
Westmoreland County, VA 26, 28
While You Were Sleeping 29
Williamsburg, VA 43
Wimbledon 28
Wolf Trap National Park for the Performing Arts 42
World War I 25
World War II 25

Y

Yorktown, VA 21